ROYAL C

Royal

TH

by Cl

First pe ... don
on 1 Oc

THE WI ... 4,
a Genes

Cumbria

COUNTY COUNCIL

Heritage Services
LIBRARIES

This book is due for return on or before the last date above.
It may be renewed by personal application, post or telephone,
if not in dema

C.L. 18F

D1407436

Royal Court Theatre presents

THE WEATHER

Clare Pollard

First performance at the Royal Court Theatre Upstairs, Sloane Square, London
on October 2004

THE WEATHER is presented as part of the YOUNG PLAYWRIGHTS' SEASON 200
Schools Project

THE WEATHER

by **Clare Pollard**

Cast in order of appearance

Daughter **Nathalie Press**
Dad **Jonathan Coy**
Mother **Helen Schlesinger**
Maria **Mia Soteriou**
Frank **Alex Robertson**

Director **Ramin Gray**
Designer **Ultz**
Lighting Designers **Ultz, Gavin Owen**
Sound Designer **Emma Laxton**
Casting **Amy Ball**
Production Manager **Sue Bird**
Stage Managers **Paul Bamford, Ella-May McDermott**
Costume Supervisors **Iona Kenrick, Jackie Orton**
Company Voice Work **Patsy Rodenburg**

The Royal Court would like to thank the following for their help with this production: Aubic Bath Supplies, www.sexshop365.co.uk, The Silk Flower Shop.

THE COMPANY

Clare Pollard (writer)
The Weather is Clare Pollard's first play.
Poetry collections include: The Heavy-Petting Zoo
(Bloodaxe, 1998) Bedtime (Bloodaxe, 2002).
Television includes: The Sixteenth Summer
(Channel 4).

Jonathan Coy
Theatre includes: Democracy (RNT); Neville's Island
(Apollo); A Midsummer Night's Dream (Almeida);
Katherine Howard (Chichester); According to
Hoyle, The Fastest Clock in the Universe, The
Philanderer, Hedda Gabler (Hampstead); Keyboard
Skills, Making Noise Quietly (Bush).
Television includes: Heartbeat, Born and Bred,
Foyle's War, Down to Earth, Hornblower, Shipman,
Midsomer Murders, Plain Jane, Nicholas Nickleby,
Falkland's Play, Longitude, The Scarlet Pimpernel,
The Adventures of Jules Verne, Touch of Frost,
Underworld, Holding On, Annie's Bar, The Rector's
Wife, Middlemarch, Henry Pratt, Inspector Morse,
Northanger Abbey, Silas Marner, Rumpole of the
Bailey, Brideshead Revisited.
Film includes: The Lost Prince, To Kill a King,
Shoreditch, Conspiracy, The Wolves of Willoughby
Chase, Maschenka.

Ramin Gray (director)
For the Royal Court: Ladybird, Advice to Iraqi
Women, Terrorism, Night Owls, Just a Bloke, Push
Up, How I Ate a Dog.
Other theatre includes: The Child, The Invisible
Woman (Gate); Cat and Mouse (Sheep) (Théâtre
National de l'Odéon, Paris/Gate); Autumn and
Winter (Man in the Moon); A Message for the
Broken-Hearted (Liverpool Playhouse and BAC); At
Fifty She Discovered the Sea, Harry's Bag, Pig's Ear,
A View from the Bridge (Liverpool Playhouse); The
Malcontent (Latchmere).
Ramin is an Associate Director of the Royal Court.

Emma Laxton (sound designer)
For the Royal Court: Bone, Food Chain, Terrorism.
Other theatre includes: My Dad is a Birdman (Young
Vic), Party Time/One For The Road (BAC); As You
Like It, Romeo and Juliet (Regent's Park Open Air
Theatre).
Emma was Head of Sound at Regent's Park Open
Air Theatre in 2001 and 2002 where projects
included; A Midsummer Night's Dream, Love's
Labours Lost, Where's Charley, The Pirates Of
Penzance, Oh! What A Lovely War.
Emma has recently been on sabbatical at the
National Theatre working with Complicite on
Measure For Measure.
Emma is Sound Deputy at the Royal Court.

Gavin Owen (lighting designer)
For the Royal Court: Imprint, Worker's Writes
As Associate Lighting Designer: Hitchcock Blo
(and Lyric); Lucky Dog.
Other theatre includes: Cross Purpose (Union
Theatre); The Matchgirls, Mack and Mabel (Pal
Theatre, Watford); Splinters, My Passionate Ma
(Massa Dance Co); Blue Murder and Jackknife
(Telltale Theatre Co).

Nathalie Press
Television includes: Brief Lives, Silent Witness,
With Me.
Film includes: My Summer of Love.
Short films include: Wasp, Mercy, Love Itchy, Sp
Rampage.
Awards include: Micahel Powell Award Edinbur
2004 for My Summer of Love, Best Actress for
Wasp at the Stockholm International Film Fes
St Petersburg and Majorca Film Festivals.

Alex Robertson
Theatre includes: The Soldier (Roman Eagle Lo
Edinburgh).
Alex has just graduated from RADA.

Helen Schlesinger
Theatre includes: Messiah (Old Vic); Uncle Vany
A Moon for the Misbegotten, King Lear, The Ill
Road to Mecca (Royal Exchange); The Oresteia
Inadmissable Evidence (RNT); The Merchant of
Venice, Twelfth Night (RSC); Mill on the Floss, V
and Peace (Shared Experience/RNT); An Inspe
Calls, Becket (RNT/West End); No Experience
Required (Hampstead); Foreign Lads (Wolsey,
Ipswich); The Europeans (Greenwich and tour)
Winters Tale, The Second Mrs Tanqueray (Salis
Miss Julie (Plymouth); Wild Oats (West Yorkshi
Playhouse); Design for Living, Don Juan (Harro
Hamlet, Romeo and Juliet, Volpone, The Tempes
(Compass Theatre).
Television includes: Dirty War, Waking the Dea
The Playground, Rose and Maloney, The Way W
Live Now, Bad Girls, The Greatest Store in the
World, Devil's Advocate, Between the Lines,
Harnessing Peacocks, Bad Girl.
Awards include: Best Actress in Manchester Ev
News Theatre Awards 2001 (A Moon for the
Misbegotten, Uncle Vanya).

Mia Soteriou

For the Royal Court: Jack, The Arbor, Young Writers' Festival, Sergeant Ola, Bed of Roses (& Bush/Hull Truck).

Theatre includes: The Two Gentlemen of Verona (Northcott Exeter); Henry IV Part 1, Henry IV Part 11 (Bristol Old Vic); Broken Glass (West Yorkshire Playhouse); The Comic Mysteries, The Government Inspector, Cyrano de Bergerac (Greenwich); School for Wives (ETT); Black Sail, White Sail (Gate/tour); Celestina (ATC tour); Eva and the Cabin Boy, Don Quixote, (Croydon Warehouse); The Magic Carpet (RNT); Pinocchio (Stratford East); Spring Awakening (Crucible, Sheffield); Lennon (Crucible, Sheffield/ Everyman, Liverpool and West End); The Venetian Twins (Nuffield, Southampton); Crime and Punishment, The White Glove (Lyric, Hammersmith); Stags and Hens (Liverpool Playhouse); 1984-Like, Blood Red Roses, Brown Bitter Wet Nellies and Scouse, Old King Cole (Everyman, Liverpool); Arabian Nights, The Merchant of Venice (Shared Experience).

Television includes: Like Father Like Son, Eastenders, TLC, Daniel Deronda, Harringham Harker, Merseybeat, MacReady and Daughter, Holby City, Kid in the Corner, Maisie Raine, Sunburn, Peak Practice, Where the Heart Is, Soldier Soldier, Casualty, The Bill, Absolutely Fabulous, The Chief, Murder Most Horrid, Smith and Jones, Blind Justice, Brookside, Queen of Hearts, Gaskin.

Film includes: Pure, Topsy Turvy, Secrets and Lies, In Hitler's Shadow, Can I Help You?, The French Lieutenant's Woman.

Radio: Mia has been a member of the BBC Radio Company.

Mia is a composer, musician, singer and songwriter. Composition includes: West End, National, RSC, Manchester Royal Exchange, Chichester Festival Theatre, Globe, Greenwich, BBC Radio, Channel 4 and Discovery TV.

She recently sang for the film Troy.

Ultz (designer and lighting designer)

As designer, for the Royal Court: Young Playwrights' Season 2004, Fallout, The Night Heron, Fireface, Lift Off, Mojo (also at Steppenwolf Theatre, Chicago).

As designer, theatre includes: sixteen productions for the RSC including Good (also on Broadway), The Art of Success (also at Manhattan Theatre Club); The Black Prince, Me and Mamie O'Rourke, A Madhouse in Goa, Animal Crackers, When Harry Met Sally (West End); Slavs! (Hampstead); The Resistible Rise of Arturo Ui, Ramayana (RNT); Hobsons Choice (Young Vic); Xerxes, La Clemenza di Tito, The Rakes Progress, Die Entführung aus dem Serail (Bavarian State Opera).

As director and designer, other theatre includes: Summer Holiday (Blackpool Opera House, London Apollo, UK tour, South African tour); Jesus Christ Superstar (Aarhus and Copenhagen); Don Giovanni, Cosi Fan Tutte (in Japanese for Tokyo Globe); A Midsummer Night's Dream (National Arts Centre, Ottawa); Dragon (RNT); The Screens (California); The Maids, Deathwatch (co-directed RSC); The Blacks (co-directed Market Theatre Johannesburg and Stockholms Stadsteater); Perikles (Stockholms Stadsteater); Snowbull (Hampstead); L'Elisir D'Amore (Tiroler Landes Theater); The Public, The Taming of the Shrew, Pericles, Baiju Bawra, Da Boyz (Theatre Royal, Stratford East).

YOUNG WRITERS PROGRAMME

The Royal Court's Young Writers Programme is committed to finding the next generation of new playwrights. Opportunities include playwriting courses for anyone between the ages of 13 and 25, play development through one to one work and rehearsed readings, pre- and post-show workshops for groups and students and special in-service training days for teachers.

Over the past two years the Young Writers Programme have led writers' groups at the Royal Court and throughout London, working with a range of young people. They have run residencies with partner theatres in Edinburgh, Liverpool, Truro and Manchester. In total the Young Writers Programme have run 415 playwriting workshops, and by January 2004 they had received 549 new plays from all over the world.

YOUNG PLAYWRIGHTS' SEASON is a Genesis Project

The Royal Court Young Writers Programme:
Associate Director **Ola Animashawun**
Administrator **Nina Lyndon**
Outreach Workers **Lucy Dunkerley, Jane Bodie**
Education Officer **Emily McLaughlin**
Writers Tutor **Simon Stephens**
Trainee Associate Director **Joe Hill-Gibbins**

THE ENGLISH STAGE COMPANY AT THE ROYAL COURT

The English Stage Company at the Royal Court opened in 1956 as a subsidised theatre producing new British plays, international plays and some classical revivals.

The first artistic director George Devine aimed to create a writers' theatre, 'a place where the dramatist is acknowledged as the fundamental creative force in the theatre and where the play is more important than the actors, the director, the designer'. The urgent need was to find a contemporary style in which the play, the acting, direction and design are all combined. He believed that 'the battle will be a long one to continue to create the right conditions for writers to work in'.

Devine aimed to discover 'hard-hitting, uncompromising writers whose plays are stimulating, provocative and exciting'. The Royal Court production of John Osborne's Look Back in Anger in May 1956 is now seen as the decisive starting point of modern British drama and the policy created a new generation of British playwrights. The first wave included John Osborne, Arnold Wesker, John Arden, Ann Jellicoe, N F Simpson and Edward Bond. Early seasons included new international plays by Bertolt Brecht, Eugène Ionesco, Samuel Beckett, Jean-Paul Sartre and Marguerite Duras.

The theatre started with the 400-seat proscenium arch Theatre Downstairs, and in 1969 opened a second theatre, the 60-seat studio Theatre Upstairs. Some productions transfer to the West End, such as Terry Johnson's Hitchcock Blonde, Caryl Churchill's Far Away, Conor McPherson's The Weir, Kevin Elyot's Mouth to Mouth and My Night With Reg. The Royal Court also co-produces plays which have transferred to the West End or toured internationally, such as Sebastian Barry's The Steward of Christendom and Mark Ravenhill's Shopping and Fucking (with Out of Joint), Martin McDonagh's The Beauty Queen Of Leenane (with Druid Theatre Company), Ayub Khan Din's East is East (with Tamasha Theatre Company, and now a feature film).

Since 1994 the Royal Court's artistic policy has again been vigorously directed to finding and producing a new generation of playwrights. The writers include Joe Penhall, Rebecca Prichard, Michael Wynne, Nick Grosso, Judy Upton, Meredith Oakes, Sarah Kane, Anthony Neilson, Judith Johnson, James Stock, Jez Butterworth, Marina Carr, Phyllis Nagy, Simon Block, Martin McDonagh, Mark Ravenhill, Ayub Khan Din, Tamantha Hammerschlag, Jess Walters, Ché Walker, Conor McPherson,

photo: Andy Chopping

Simon Stephens, Richard Bean, Roy Williams, Gary Mitchell, Mick Mahoney, Rebecca Gilman, Christopher Shinn, Kia Corthron, David Gieselmann, Marius von Mayenburg, David Eldridge, Leo Butler, Zinnie Harris, Grae Cleugh, Roland Schimmelpfennig, DeObia Oparei, Enda Walsh, Vassily Sigarev, the Presnyakov Brothers, Marcos Barbosa, Lucy Prebble and John Donnelly. This expanded programme of new plays has been made possible through the support of A.S.K. Theater Projects and the Skirball Foundation, The Jerwood Charity, the American Friends of the Royal Court Theatre and many in association with the National Theatre Studio.

In recent years there have been record-breaking productions at the box office, with capacity houses for Roy Williams' Fallout, Terry Johnson's Hitchcock Blonde, Caryl Churchill's A Number, Jez Butterworth's The Night Heron, Rebecca Gilman's Boy Gets Girl, Kevin Elyot's Mouth to Mouth, David Hare's My Zinc Bed and Conor McPherson's The Weir, which transferred to the West End in October 1998 and ran for nearly two years at the Duke of York's Theatre.

The newly refurbished theatre in Sloane Square opened in February 2000, with a policy still inspired by the first artistic director George Devine. The Royal Court is an international theatre for new plays and new playwrights, and the work shapes contemporary drama in Britain and overseas.

AWARDS FOR ROYAL COURT

Jez Butterworth won the 1995 George Devine Award, the Writers' Guild New Writer of the Year Award, the Evening Standard Award for Most Promising Playwright and the Olivier Award for Best Comedy for Mojo.

The Royal Court was the overall winner of the 1995 Prudential Award for the Arts for creativity, excellence, innovation and accessibility. The Royal Court Theatre Upstairs won the 1995 Peter Brook Empty Space Award for innovation and excellence in theatre.

Michael Wynne won the 1996 Meyer-Whitworth Award for The Knocky. Martin McDonagh won the 1996 George Devine Award, the 1996 Writers' Guild Best Fringe Play Award, the 1996 Critics' Circle Award and the 1996 Evening Standard Award for Most Promising Playwright for The Beauty Queen of Leenane. Marina Carr won the 19th Susan Smith Blackburn Prize (1996/7) for Portia Coughlan. Conor McPherson won the 1997 George Devine Award, the 1997 Critics' Circle Award and the 1997 Evening Standard Award for Most Promising Playwright for The Weir. Ayub Khan Din won the 1997 Writers' Guild Awards for Best West End Play and Writers' Guild New Writer of the Year and the 1996 John Whiting Award for East is East (co-production with Tamasha).

At the 1998 Tony Awards, Martin McDonagh's The Beauty Queen of Leenane (co-production with Druid Theatre Company) won four awards including Garry Hynes for Best Director and was nominated for a further two. Eugene Ionesco's The Chairs (co-production with Theatre de Complicite) was nominated for six Tony awards. David Hare won the 1998 Time Out Live Award for Outstanding Achievement and six awards in New York including the Drama League, Drama Desk and New York Critics Circle Award for Via Dolorosa. Sarah Kane won the 1998 Arts Foundation Fellowship in Playwriting. Rebecca Prichard won the 1998 Critics' Circle Award for Most Promising Playwright for Yard Gal (co-production with Clean Break).

Conor McPherson won the 1999 Olivier Award for Best New Play for The Weir. The Royal Court won the 1999 ITI Award for Excellence in International Theatre. Sarah Kane's Cleansed was judged Best Foreign Language Play in 1999 by Theater Heute in Germany. Gary Mitchell won the 1999 Pearson Best Play Award for Trust. Rebecca Gilman was joint winner of the 1999 George Devine Award and won the 1999 Evening Standard Award for Most Promising Playwright for The Glory of Living.

In 1999, the Royal Court won the European theatre prize New Theatrical Realities, presented at Taormina Arte in Sicily, for its efforts in recent years in discovering and producing the work of young British dramatists.

Roy Williams and Gary Mitchell were joint winners of the George Devine Award 2000 for Most Promising Playwright for Lift Off and The Force of Change respectively. At the Barclays Theatre Awards 2000 presented by the TMA, Richard Wilson won the Best Director Award for David Gieselmann's Mr Kolpert and Jeremy Herbert won the Best Designer Award for Sarah Kane's 4.48 Psychosis. Gary Mitchell won the Evening Standard's Charles Wintour Award 2000 for Most Promising Playwright for The Force of Change. Stephen Jeffreys' I Just Stopped by to See the Man won an AT&T: On Stage Award 2000.

David Eldridge's Under the Blue Sky won the Time Out Live Award 2001 for Best New Play in the West End. Leo Butler won the George Devine Award 2001 for Most Promising Playwright for Redundant. Roy Williams won the Evening Standard's Charles Wintour Award 2001 for Most Promising Playwright for Clubland. Grae Cleugh won the 2001 Olivier Award for Most Promising Playwright for Fucking Games. Richard Bean was joint winner of the George Devine Award 2002 for Most Promising Playwright for Under the Whaleback. Caryl Churchill won the 2002 Evening Standard Award for Best New Play for A Number. Vassily Sigarev won the 2002 Evening Standard Charles Wintour Award for Most Promising Playwright for Plasticine. Ian MacNeil won the 2002 Evening Standard Award for Best Design for A Number and Plasticine. Peter Gill won the 2002 Critics' Circle Award for Best New Play for The York Realist (English Touring Theatre). Ché Walker won the 2003 George Devine Award for Most Promising Playwright for Flesh Wound. Lucy Prebble won the 2003 Critics' Circle Award and the 2004 George Devine Award for Most Promising Playwright for The Sugar Syndrome.

ROYAL COURT BOOKSHOP

The Royal Court bookshop offers a diverse selection of contemporary plays and publications on the theory and practice of modern drama. The staff specialise in assisting with the selection of audition monologues and scenes.
Royal Court playtexts from past and present productions cost £2.
The Bookshop is situated in the downstairs ROYAL COURT BAR AND FOOD.
Monday–Friday 3–10pm, Saturday 2.30–10pm
For information tel: 020 7565 5024
or email: bookshop@royalcourttheatre.com

PROGRAMME SUPPORTERS

The Royal Court (English Stage Company Ltd) receives its principal funding from Arts Council England, London. It is also supported financially by a wide range of private companies and public bodies and earns the remainder of its income from the box office and its own trading activities. The Royal Borough of Kensington & Chelsea gives an annual grant to the Royal Court Young Writers Programme.
The Genesis Foundation supports the International Season and Young Writers Festival.

The Jerwood Charity supports new plays by new playwrights through the Jerwood New Playwrights series. The Skirball Foundation funds a Playwrights' Programme at the theatre. The Artistic Director's Chair is supported by a lead grant from The Peter Jay Sharp Foundation, contributing to the activities of the Artistic Director's office. Bloomberg Mondays, the Royal Court's reduced price ticket scheme, is supported by Bloomberg. Over the past eight years the BBC has supported the Gerald Chapman Fund for directors.

THE AMERICAN FRIENDS OF THE ROYAL COURT THEATRE

AFRCT support the mission of the Royal Court and is primarily focused on raising funds to enable the theatre to produce new work by emerging American writers. Since this not-for-profit organisation was founded in 1997, AFRCT have contributed to ten productions. They have also supported the participation of young artists in the Royal Court's acclaimed International Residency.

If you would like to support the ongoing work of the Royal Court, please contact the Development Department on 020 7565 5050.

ROYAL COURT
SLOANE SQUARE

Jerwood Theatre Upstairs
YOUNG PLAYWRIGHTS' SEASON 2004

A Genesis Project

Design: Ultz

5–16 October 9.30pm
BEAR HUG
by Robin French
Directed by Ramin Gray
Cast includes: Jonathan Coy, Alex Robertson, Helen Schlesinger, and Mia Soteriou

5–20 November 7.45pm
FRESH KILLS
by Elyzabeth Gregory Wilder
Directed by Wilson Milam

26 November–18 December 7.45pm
A GIRL IN A CAR WITH A MAN
by Rob Evans
Directed by Joe Hill-Gibbins

BOX OFFICE
020 7565 5000
BOOK ONLINE
www.royalcourttheatre.com

Clare Pollard
The Weather

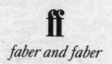

faber and faber

First published in 2004
by Faber and Faber Limited
3 Queen Square London WC1N 3AU

Typeset by Country Setting, Kingsdown, Kent CT14 8ES
Printed in England by Mackays of Chatham plc, Chatham, Kent

A CIP record for this book
is available from the British Library

ISBN 0-571-22718-X

2 4 6 8 10 9 7 5 3 1

Characters

Gail
Forties, white. Very attractive, and dresses
to maximise her sex appeal.

Bob
Fifties, white. Her husband. Wears expensive suits.

Ellie
Fifteen, white. Their daughter.
Wears only black and lots of make-up.

Maria
Forties, Spanish. Their cleaner.

Frank
Seventeen, white. Ellie's boyfriend.
Wears whatever reasonably cool teenage boys wear.

Time
The very near future

THE WEATHER

Notes

*If the poltergeist special effects are a bit awkward
and jerky with obvious strings, etc., this isn't important,
and might even add an extra level of metaphor.*

CAPITAL LETTERS
*indicate a suggested rise in volume,
though not necessarily to the level of shouting.*

*Beat
indicates a short pause, often signalling
a change of thought, tone or rhythm.*

SCENE ONE

A kitchen. Ellie sits at the table. There is a large window on the back wall, through which we can see a dark, stormy sky. Wind and rain can be heard lashing the house throughout.

Ellie It's over.

Pause.

I mean. Have you seen the weather out there? Have you seen the fucking weather?

Pause.

It's over, everyone knows it now, we're just waiting. Aren't we? (*Beat.*) Have you seen the weather? (*Beat.*) Sometimes there's storms, that crack the sky, and for days it looks punched, lavender and custard, or steel, and the rain hurts, like it wants to beat you to nothing. And knives of light – the lightning trying to cut you. (*Beat.*) Then next week, hurray, it'll be sun – except after a day or two it won't stop, we'll be swimming in the sweat of it, that rank lather of heat, and the worry'll start – it's bees, or malaria, or drought, death, ice age, we're melting. (*Beat.*) Or no, no, there'll be wind. Gales. Cities torn out by the roots, crashing fucking everything, windscreens smashing, two dead in Brighton, van swept off the motorway in Morecambe, Durham razed. Fuck. FUCK. Do they not just? Could they not? (*Beat.*) But no, it's not their fault, it's not global warming. It's natural, it's cycles, it's unproven, it's cows farting, it's China, it's probably China.

Pause.

How long do you think I'll live? Ten years? Twenty? How long before the antibiotics run out, and the UV gets me, or the terrorists, or the rogue states, the super-bugs, the floods, the panic, the panic, the panic?

Pause.

Go on, how long do you give me? You greedy fucking selfish fucks. Come on. It's over, isn't it? (*Beat.*) It's over.

Bob enters with a briefcase and umbrella. Shakes himself down like a dog. Puts down case and takes off coat, hanging it up.

Bob Have you seen the weather out there?

Ellie Yes. I'm not blind.

Bob Don't be like that, I've had a long hard day. (*Beat.*) You couldn't make me a cup of tea, could you, darling? I could kill for a cup of tea.

Pause.

Ellie I was making one anyway.

Ellie begins to make up two cups of tea.

Bob So what are you moping round in here for? Don't you have some free minutes on your phone or something?

Ellie No.

Bob You look nice. Oh, I remember. You're meeting that boy again, aren't you? I'm not sure I want you walking into town, to be honest. It's filthy out there.

Ellie He's got a car, he'll pick me up if I ask.

Bob You're a bit young, aren't you?

Ellie For what?

8

Bob A boy with a car. Be careful with him, Ellie. Don't let him force you into anything.

Ellie Don't, you sound like her.

Bob Just be careful. (*Beat.*) So I guess the fact you've not gone out yet means you haven't apologised to your mother?

Ellie I should just go out anyway.

Bob You know it's not worth it. Not the way she is at the moment. Go on. Be big about it.

Ellie Just. Can you not? I didn't do anything.

Bob I know, but.

Ellie If you know, then why don't you stand up for me for once? Can you not just stand up for me?

Bob It's a sensitive time. Keep the peace.

Ellie She's just so.

Bob I know.

Ellie She's so excessive. She has to. (*Beat.*) Paws in everything. Always poking for secrets. (*Mimics.*) 'Go on, tell me the goss. I'm your mum, I need to know the goss.'

Bob She's a bit lonely at the moment. Since, well. You know. She needs you. (*Beat.*) You're her best friend.

Ellie No I'm not Dad, I'm her fucking daughter.

Bob Don't, okay? I've had a hard day, I'm dead on my feet. It's hard for us all, you have to be responsible.

Ellie hands him his tea.

Ellie Oh yes. I forgot how responsible you are. I forgot your company –

Bob Blah, blah, come on, not this again. We all make mistakes, Ellie. I'm sick of you being such a child about it.

You need to be more – (*Beat.*) Be an adult about this. You really have no idea about the world I move in, the decisions that have to be made – jobs, wages, people's food on the table, economic growth, money, you know. (*Beat.*) Money so you can have your phone and your nice house and your trendy haircut or whatever it is and your nice state-of-the-art room –

Ellie And my nice malaria tablets, and state-of-the-art car-bombs in the town centre.

Bob I am *not* responsible for the world's woes, darling.

Ellie Yes you are.

Bob Really just. (*Slurps the tea.*) Shut up now, that was silly, I'm not having this discussion.

Ellie Yeah, well, that sounds like you.

Bob Please! Jesus. Where's your mum? Where's the TV guide?

Ellie Bed and bed with her.

Bob What, she's feeling ill again?

Ellie Well. (*Beat.*) She sloshed back some vodka, necked a handful of pills, turned ghostly, swooned a little. It depends what you mean. (*Beat.*) She's sick in the head if that's what you mean.

Bob Sweetheart. (*Beat.*) Just. I know it's a drag for you but check she's okay, bring me the TV guide. I need a little peace.

A roll of thunder and crack of lightning. Ellie drinks her tea.

Ellie Have you seen the weather?

Bob Look, I was like you. You're young, and everything seems shit, and hopeless, but it's not. You think the world's going to end, but it doesn't. You wake up expecting the bomb, the big bang, and there's nothing, there's just some celebrity shagging another celebrity behind some celebrity's back, and they were ten-times-a-night-tastic and coke fiends, or they're trying to raise our taxes again – another blow to the middle classes – or the trains aren't working. Listen, honey, the trains are NEVER working. (*Beat.*) And you're young, you want to think you can solve it, that we can be saved, or that there's someone to hate, at the least – you're full of hate – so you reckon, it's *us,* it's our society, it's Mum and Dad. They're the ones to blame. And that's so easy because you can see us, you can hate us, you can beat us up. (*Beat.*) You'll learn.

 Pause.

Listen, sweetheart, we might not be perfect, but. It's THEM, they're the ones who do the damage. They're the ones who slit a grandmother's throat. They're the ones who smash a plane into a tower block. (*Beat.*) And the older you get, the more you realise it's them. Them. The ones you don't understand, and will never. The ones you can't save. The ones you cannot stop.

 Pause.

But that's okay, they're the minority.

Ellie You *wanker.*

Bob Enough, go and check on your mum.

 Gail enters.

Oh. Evening, you.

Gail Cocktails, cocktails. I declare a . . . a *state* of cocktails. C'mon. I fancy a . . . a . . . what? What, darling daughter?

Ellie Dunno.

Pause.

White Russian?

Gail Good one, good one. I like those. I'd like that. So. Are you meeting that boy tonight then, whatsisname?

Ellie Yes, I. Yes.

Gail And?

Ellie And nothing.

Gail Come on, you've not even told me what he looks like yet. Is he hunky? Don't tell me – hair like coffee and eyes like moss? No, no. Hair like a beach, and eyes the silver of penknives . . .

Ellie Can I have a White Russian too?

Gail Okay. But I want the info. I want the goss.

Ellie *Mum.*

Gail I hope he's not got stuck in the storm. It's wild out there. (*Beat.*) I love it, I wrote a poem. (*Beat.*)

My child tastes the electrical air –
steps outside as the thick sky tears.
O daughter, dragged damp as a calf from me –
tonight may all beds be soaked,
soaked through to the skin.

Bob Love, come on.

Ellie I can't believe you wrote that.

Gail Oh, come on.

Ellie Come on!

Bob Yeah, come on, she's joking.

Gail I'm not joking, Bob. It's a fucking good poem.

Bob You've had a drink or two though, tell her you'll revise.

Gail After last night? She's lucky I'm speaking to her. (*Beat.*) What? You think two drinks makes me forget?

Ellie Two?

Gail Anyway, that's okay, I'll forget, because I love you.

Stands beside Ellie. Touches her face.

You're so beautiful. My sugarmouse. I could eat you.

Ellie (*shrugging off Gail's hand*) I'm going out.

Gail No you're not, it's too wet.

Ellie But you just said. (*Beat.*) I have to meet him.

Gail Phone him. Tell him to meet you here. White Russians. Say there's oodles of delicious, creamy White Russians.

Ellie No, you said yesterday I could go out.

Gail You said yesterday I was a vindictive, sick old FREAK. (*Beat.*) Okay? (*Beat.*) Which I think means that's final. (*Beat.*) Anyway. You make the best White Russians, go on. You have one too. Make yourself a nice strong one.

Pause.

Bob I don't like to say, really. (*Beat.*) But. It's nothing, and anyway, you're sober so. The cards. I just wondered where the credit cards were.

Gail Where did you leave them?

Bob I don't. Not sure. But, well. In my wallet I'm pretty sure, and my wallet's not been out of my pocket except –

Ellie begins to make White Russians, occasionally taking a swig of tea.

Gail Check under the bed if you want. Check the wardrobe. I haven't been on some fucking buying binge, if that's what you mean. I've been here writing. (*Beat.*) Here's some good lines for you:

> Shoes cry to me, little empty vaginas,
> Dresses whisper my name – stage curtains –
> I hand over my coin for the day's dream, mutter the
>   prayer:
> May these goods make me good,
> May these bright things make me not myself.

Pause. Touches Ellie's hair.

Listen, my peach, listen, I just want to know if you've kissed him yet. It's a big moment for my baby. That's all. I remember my first kiss, in a cinema, just after this blonde goddess and this smart guy – plain, but, you know, funny and nice, a writer type – had finally said 'I love you' in the rain. It hissed so loudly, the whole cinema was spilling with it. And everything was so big, and the colours of jukeboxes and Florida, so bright. And I thought – that's what my life will be like. When I get out of this town. When I can do what I want. When I kiss him. That's how things will look when I have Love. (*Beat.*) He wasn't the one of course, he was just this boy, with hot dog on his breath, and a soft cold mouth, and I think I knew that already, but still. (*Beat.*) It's a big moment for a girl. Sort of like this peak of hope. (*Beat. Laughingly*) Your first *fingering* on the other hand . . .

Ellie Don't.

Gail kisses her forehead, lingeringly. Whispers into her brow:

Gail Joke, joke.

Ellie That dress is new.

Gail No it's not.

Ellie The tags. I see your tags.

Pause.

Gail Okay, fine. Cooking time. Chef's time. And tonight, monsieur and madame, I shall prepare . . . (*Looks in fridge.*) Pork chops and peas.

Bob Fine. Good.

Ellie I'll get takeaway with him.

Gail No, dinner first, proper dinner, not bowelburgers and chickenshit kebabs. (*Beat.*) Now. Peas! Peas, please.

Bob I'll do it, darling.

Gail No that's fine, you should be looking for your cards, I'm sure they're here somewhere. That is, unless you want to check my panties.

Bob Come on.

Gail (*laughing*) Hey, don't say I don't fucking try! Have you seen the weather?

Bob Mmm, pork chops should be nice.

Ellie What about if I go out after dinner, in an hour?

Bob We'll see about the weather.

Ellie pours out White Russians.

Gail Does he have any moles, or birthmarks. Or little quirks, you know? Tetanus scar. Trace of a harelip . . . (*Beat.*) My tip – read any poet, any, they home in on the flaws. Tell him you adore the way his belly button sticks out, or his lazy eye or something, he's yours.

Ellie What was Dad's weakness?

15

Gail Gold card.

Ellie He. (*Beat.*) This boy's normal, okay, not some weirdo poet.

Gail Sounds boring.

Ellie passes round the White Russians. They all drink. Gail is left with a thick white moustache.

Bob I had a hard day at work.

Gail No shit?

Bob That's really nice.

Gail Yeah, well.

Bob She was right, you are drunk.

Ellie Oh that's right, Dad, get me involved.

Gail necks the whole glass of White Russian and slams it down on the table.

Gail You involve yourself, you prissy fucking holy cow.

Ellie You're so, *so* horrible.

Gail shrugs.

That's it? That's IT?

Bob Come on now, love. (*Beat.*) Don't start. Maybe you should go out now.

Ellie Did you not hear her? Is that all you can say? (*Beat.*) You do nothing, ever, nothing. It's pitiful, that's what it is. It's pathetic.

Bob Please, can we just have some maturity here?

Ellie No, why should I? I hate you, Dad. I HATE YOU.

Gail (*as the emptied glass slowly drags its way to the edge of the worktop*) Well. Nothing like a nice *family*

evening, is there? Now top up my glass would you, love,
I could do with another stiff drink –

*The glass hurls itself off with an almighty smash. They
jump violently.*

Blackout.

SCENE TWO

*The kitchen again. Gail sits at the kitchen table sipping a
Martini, whilst Maria cleans. There are piles of shopping
bags on the floor. Through the window, which is open,
we can see a hot blue sky, and a dazzle of sun. A fan
standing in the corner hums throughout.*

Gail I'm telling you, Maria, it was scary, it scared the shit
out of me. (*Beat.*) And hubby keeps telling me there's a
normal explanation, of course, dullard that he is. (*Beat.*)
He's lying though. He's always lying. Christ, he must lie
nearly as much as me. (*Beat.*) Ever since it happened, I can
feel it in the house – licking its ears behind the fridge,
touching the back of my neck in the shower, leaving its
shape on the bed – something. Something evil. This morning, a door banged open. *Bang.* And not even a breeze.

Maria crosses herself.

I shouldn't be telling you really, should I, when you have
to work here? (*Beat.*) *And* our cards have gone missing,
he blames me of course. Pass me the thingy, would you?

Maria passes the cocktail shaker.

Maria There you are.

Gail decants another Martini into her glass.

Gail And my daughter knows something too. She won't
say, but I can see she feels it as well. That judder when

17

I put my hand on her arm. (*Beat.*) I couldn't sleep last night. And then this morning I was in such a shape, I thought. I thought I'd go shopping – I still had some store cards. I went to the mall and, as soon as I walked in, this stillness fell on me – do you know what I mean? The chandelier and the glass elevator swooshing people up and down. I know my husband says they're unsafe now, but I just don't think anything bad could happen there. It's like a cathedral. (*Beat.*) I bought a cashmere throw, stupid. I mean the heat. Have you felt the heat? (*Beat.*) But it was so soft, like a boxful of kittens, so unnecessarily beautiful. And then I bought a red swimsuit, and a fat, red leather journal to match it. Yellow roses. Three good, bloody steaks. Lapsang souchong . . .

  Pause.

And suddenly, it was all. (*Beat.*) Beautiful. I would come back and put the yellow roses in a vase in the kitchen, and throw the windows open to all that glorious light, and drink cocktails and dance in my red swimsuit. I really did feel hopeful, Maria –

  Pause.

I'm manic, that's what my therapist says. I feel very intensely. Too much! Too much. When I came back, you see, I noticed that the kettle had changed places with the toaster, and I knew it was – *it* – and now look at me shaking again.

Maria Oh, I'm sorry, I must have moved it, cleaning.

Gail You! (*Beat.*) Ha.

Maria I'm so, so sorry.

Gail Fine, fine. Don't in future, though, or how will I know? (*Swigs drink.*) Eh?

Maria I don't know.

Gail How ridiculous! You must think I'm ridiculous!

Pause.

The sun, though. The sun. I used to worship the sun. (*Beat.*) When I was young I'd lie out for hours, until my legs and my arms were café au lait, all loose and smooth with heat. Taking its life in. (*Beat.*) I know they say it kills now, but some days I think they're just spoiling my fun.

Maria They thought my sister's cancer was from sunburn.

Gail That's a shame.

Maria That week I took off last year, for the funeral.

Gail Life is hard. I wish I could lose myself. A fling. I'd like to be flung. Remember Alistair?

Maria Yes, I remember Alistair.

Gail How you'd have to clean his cups and ash away, and make the bed, before . . . (*Beat.*) You were a good liar. It was fun. (*Beat.*) Maybe I could phone him. (*Beat.*) God, he knew how to *do* things with his tongue . . .

Pause.

No. No. That's all gone now, isn't it? Those days. I'm getting older, Maria. My eyes are scored. My neck sags like chicken skin. I can taste the rot on my gums. (*Beat.*) No more romance for me – no more secret, perfumed letters, bodies pressed to wall, fishnets baggying round ankles, late-night calls, just. (*Beat.*) Diminishment. The world becoming less every day.

Maria You're not *so* old.

Gail My daughter is a woman now.

Pause. She finishes the Martini, stands and starts mixing another one.

I'm old and I never found true love, not really. Too late now. I wonder if they lied. I wonder if there's any such thing.

Bob enters carrying briefcase. Puts it down.

Bob Any such what?

Gail Martini? (*Remembers all the shopping bags.*) Whoops!

Bob What the – what are these, darling?

Gail Things.

Pause.

Nice things.

Bob You don't even have any *cards*.

Gail Store cards. It's okay. No interest until next year. Air miles.

Bob You can't.

Gail It's okay. Buy now pay later.

Bob You can't keep doing this, love.

Pause.

Gail Do you even remember what happened to me last month? It makes me feel better. It makes me feel happy. It makes me feel NEW. (*Beat.*) I would have thought it was a slight cost for –

Bob Slight! You – you *idiot*. Everything through our door these last few weeks has had red edges. I got a letter today. Some card's passing us on to debt collectors and I have no money. I've moved money from one card to another card to another, but they won't give me any more cards, and they'll come round here and take our things. (*Beat.*) Do you understand? (*Beat.*) If you don't stop spending they'll take *all our things*.

Pause.

Gail I just. (*Beat.*) I just don't need this guilt and stress right now. I can't handle it. (*Beat.*) It's so hot in here, I'm hot and bothered. (*Beat.*) Have you felt the heat?

Pause.

I just thought I deserved something, okay? I just thought I deserved some nice things. (*She begins to shake the shaker, getting progressively more violent until abruptly stopping at the end of this speech.*) I'm so fucking depressed, don't you get that? I wake up, and it's like everything's dead and clichéd. And I feel like frozen meat. And I walk in the bathroom and everything's – my foundation smells stale and I've got silver hairs in my pubes. And my daughter upstairs hates me and keeps secrets, even though all I do is love her, and you sleep with your back turned to me, and when you kiss me it's like. It's like when you swallow your multivitamin. (*Beat.*) And my writing's dried up and if I died. If I died I reckon it would shoot up the charts again. There'd be big, gushing obituaries in the papers, with photos of me when I was twenty and sexy and still had a hope –

Bob Sweetheart, I. (*Beat.*) I'm trying, I'm trying, but the spending, we can't –

Notices Maria is standing watching.

Could you leave actually, Maria? This is private.

Gail She's involved too.

Bob Just. Sorry, Maria. Could you maybe put the hose on? The garden's parched.

Maria Hose ban. The papers say it's the beginning of a drought. The worst drought ever. (*Beat.*) Terrible, terrible drought.

Bob You shouldn't read the papers. (*Beat.*) Well then, maybe clean the latrines, Maria. I don't think they've been cleaned all that recently.

Maria Sorry, but I cleaned the – the *latrines* this morning.

Bob Oh.

Gail Christ, why beat around the bush? Why not just get her to warm my pearls?

Bob Will you not undermine me? Please.

Maria Excuse me, but you think can't afford me any more?

Bob Oh no, Maria, we can afford *you*, you're virtually family. Just not luxuries.

  Pause.

Maria I think maybe. (*Beat.*) Maybe *High-Hope Hospice* might be on the TV, I sometimes watch it while I iron.

Bob Iron! Yes. Fantastic.

  She leaves. Gail pours out two Martinis. Gives one to Bob.

Gail Cheers. (*Beat.*) Here's to – happiness! Here's to the sun!

Bob I'm trying my best. I am trying. (*Beat.*) I'm going to ask my mother for a loan tomorrow, I know you aren't keen but –

Gail Oh, she'll love that.

Bob She won't *love* that, actually, she'd probably much rather keep the money herself, so don't be –

Gail You know she hates me. You know she thinks I'm a shit mother. Ever since I went in with postnatal depression and she had to help out. She thinks I'm unnatural.

Bob She doesn't.

Gail You are so. (*Beat.*) Fuck, you'll pretend not to see anything to avoid taking sides, won't you?

Pause.

Christ, you even pretended not to see the poltergeist!

Bob Poltergeist! When did it become a poltergeist! One smashed cup!

Gail Things have been moving, Bob.

Bob We have a CLEANER!

Gail I can sense it, I can SENSE it, I can feel it everywhere in the house, something OTHER, something –

The toaster begins to lift up off the worktop.

It scares me, it scares me, and you won't even admit you SAW it!

Bob Will you just snap out of this! I had a tough day at work and –

The toaster swings for his head. He ducks. Gail screams and scrambles under the table. The toaster drops. The windows slam shut.

What the hell?

Gail Oh God oh God oh God.

The sound of feet running down steps. Ellie enters.

Ellie What happened? What happened?

Gail Careful!

Ellie WHAT?

Bob It was a. God.

Ellie Was it. It?

Bob The toaster lifted up, and flew across – flew at my head.

Gail It was *here* again. It's in our house. Careful, lamb!

Pause.

Ellie Nothing's happening.

Bob It must have gone.

Gail gets out gingerly from under the table. Lights a cigarette.

Gail We'll have to move, I can't live here.

Bob We can't afford to move. (*Beat.*) Maybe my mother –

Gail No FUCKING way.

Ellie HELLO, WHO IS IT? ARE YOU THERE? SPEAK TO ME.

Gail *Don't.* (*Beat.*) We need an exorcist.

Ellie There is no God. How can he help? (*Beat.*) COME OUT, COME OUT, WHOEVER YOU ARE.

Gail Don't. (*Beat.*) I'm scared, I'm scared.

Bob Don't be scared.

Gail (*becoming tearful*) It's *scary* though. It was trying to hurt us. Didn't you see it? It wants to hurt us.

Bob Hey, darling. (*Touches her shoulder.*) There, there.

Ellie Can I have a Martini?

Bob Yeah, go on then.

Gail pours herself a vodka. Drinks some.

Ellie I'm glad I'm going out tonight.

Gail You're going out?

Ellie I told you, to his place.

Gail I don't want you out, we need to be together, a family. Tell him to come round here.

Ellie No, Mum.

Gail He's more important than your family? (*Beat.*) Oh, I see.

Ellie What do you see?

Gail You think you're in love, don't you? You think this little stud's the one. Always banging on every night about having to see him. So go on, what makes him so special? What differentiates him from all the other losers you've brought home? His sensitivity? His puppy-plop eyes? Melt my heart and maybe I'll let you go out. (*Beat.*) Well?

Ellie He gets me away from you, that's all.

Gail Oh, that's nice! That's romance. You must get that romantic side from your father.

Ellie He wants to work in New York next year. I might go with him.

Bob cautiously picks up the toaster and puts it back.

Bob Ellie, love, don't provoke her.

Gail We'd better meet him then, hadn't we? If you're going to go off gallivanting.

Ellie I am not bringing him here to get a fucking kettle in the head, okay? (*Beat.*) Anyway, I know what you're like.

25

Gail What am I like?

Ellie Just . . .

Gail No. No, go on.

Ellie Well, at best you'll start quoting poetry, or more likely you'll be like with the last two boys I brought back, heavy breathing in their ears, slicking your lips, making suggestive remarks about the vegetables we're having for tea or whatever. You can't. (*Beat.*) You hate me having anything for myself. (*Beat.*) This time it'll probably be like: 'Oh, I'm so frightened, can you hold me?' then trying to work out if he's got an erection.

Gail Oh. Right. I see. (*Pause.*) Tell you what, honeypuff, make me another Martini and I'll quote some more poetry.

> I wither, I winter.
> Beneath the moon's toilet bowl
> my daughter struts in my pale skin,
> as though it was never a gift –
> cries thief when I try to touch.

Ellie You better fucking not have written that.

Gail It's my art.

Ellie It's – (*Beat.*) For fuck's sake, Mum, it's ME. ME.

Gail You're my daughter. I'm supposed to pretend you're not part of my life?

Ellie Carry this on and I WON'T be.

Gail Oh, that's right, you'll be with loverboy, tonguing on top of the Empire State. Get a grip Ellie, it's embarrassing.

Bob Do we have to have this again? A toaster, for crying out loud! A toaster almost killed me.

Ellie looks around at the bags.

Ellie For fuck's sake, Mum, not again? Look at all this crap!

Gail It's not crap.

Ellie You're such a selfish bitch.

Gail Selfish!

Ellie You said I couldn't go on holiday with the others. You said we couldn't afford it, hard times coming up, belt-tightening, and all *this*.

Gail I'm ILL. Does nobody around here give me any leeway?

Ellie rummages through the bags.

Ellie All shit, all packaging, all plastic and paper and labels, all little kids' fingers worked to blood in dirty sweatshops, all chemically pumped calves and shafted, starving farmers, and the corpses of whales and tigers and dolphins, and unfair sanctions and hate and greed, greed, greed –

Gail My daughter the fucking hippy.

Ellie holds up coffee.

Ellie This isn't even fair trade! I asked you to get me fair trade. It fucking matters to me. I know you think it's shit and you don't care, but it matters. To. Me.

Gail Sorry. Sorry.

Ellie No you're not. If you were you'd remember.

Gail Next time. Okay? Next time, I promise.

Ellie You don't give a shit about anything but *you* – your feelings, your art, your appetites, your precious depression –

Gail LEAVE ME ALONE.

Ellie THERE'S NOTHING I'D LIKE BETTER.

Bob Come on now. Come on, give your mother a break. You know she's. At the moment. (*Beat.*) I'm out there all day, slaving my guts out for you two, so you can live in the style to which. (*Beat.*) It's hard times, with the terrorism. Business is scared. They're laying jobs off. It's not here yet, not yet, but if we have a Santa Monica here, just even the suggestion of a bomb in a mall like that, can you imagine? (*Beat.*) People don't enjoy shopping like they did already – and I know I'm supposed to say it's cool, it's fine, never again, but – I mean, that's *another* reason I don't like your mother shopping all the time.

   Pause.

They're out there, now. Them. *Them.* And I come home, wanting to relax, a drink, dinner, time with my girls, and there's all this screaming and hate, and now. Now this. (*Beat.*) There must be a rational explanation. (*Beat.*) Maybe if we reason with it. (*Beat.*) Maybe there's something on the internet.

Ellie Yeah, Dad. Hey, I know! Maybe it will just go away.

   Blackout.

SCENE THREE

The kitchen. Ellie is sitting at the table, drinking whisky from a tumbler. Through the window snow is softly falling. The word PERVERT *is scrawled messily on the wall.*

Ellie It's over.

   Pause.

28

I mean, have you heard the news? Have you heard the fucking news? Three malls in one day. The sales. Two thousand dead, and we saw the pictures, the shaky CCTV, all the people sweating and crushing, awkward with armfuls of holiday bikini and bargain-bin nighties and end-of-line flip-flops and picnic sets and skirts. All wanting to make things nice, make things special. Cheer themselves up. Have a treat. All those people queuing at the cash tills and pushing their plastic across the counters, sign here. (*Beat.*) BOOM!

Pause.

They're so scared, the politicians. And it's just the start, they know it. Think about it, if they're targeting capitalism . . . Garages, spas, burger bars, supermarkets, power stations, machines that dispense cola – there's panic. There's hysteria. People are going loopy.

Pause.

BOOM!

Pause.

There were people splattered with webs of blood, people howling like dogs. Really *howling*. And so many dead bodies – like mannequins. Or just the arms of mannequins sometimes, plastic bags full of goodies still looped over their wrists. It was like a fucking war zone, like somewhere in the Middle East or something. (*Beat.*) And then it started to snow. Snow, for fuck's sake! People shivering and screaming in the wet of it, trying to shelter the injured with half-price sun-hats. (*Beat.*) They're saying: 'Dark day for the economy.' They're saying, 'Life savings lost.' My father's job probably. My mother's hobby. (*Beat.*) Sorry, my mother's fucking *addiction*.

Pause. The whisky bottle lifts, tilts and pours her another drink.

Oh, you again. You. Will you not just. (*Beat.*) Oh God, can it not stop?

Gail enters.

Gail We need to talk.

Ellie Oh.

Gail I'm frightened, sweetpea, your father's job . . .

Ellie He'll find another.

Gail But we owe money. Oh, it's my fault, I know. Everything I touch turns rancid. I wish I was dead.

Ellie Don't do this.

Gail We owe money and they're going to take our things. And your father's so mad, I think he's angry at me. He's going to leave me and I don't know what I'll do.

Ellie Don't.

Gail pours herself a whisky.

Gail This poltergeist is the last straw. I can't sleep. I dream it's lying on top of me, cool and damp and smothering, with this horrible spiced sweat smell, like Africa, or it's holding a blade to my throat, or it's walking into the bedroom with this bomb strapped to it, and we're all going to die. (*Beat.*) Sugarplum, about this poltergeist. (*Beat.*) I was talking to Maria, and she said. She said she saw on daytime TV that they've found in almost all houses with poltergeists, there's a teenage girl, and I looked it up on the computer, and she's right, they say. Well one theory is that it's to do with a daughter's *anger*.

Ellie Oh God, you're not going to blame it on me?

Gail I'm just saying.

Ellie You're such a fucking unbelievable cow.

30

Gail Must you be so *nasty* to me?

Ellie Don't.

Gail You're angry, I know you're angry, but I try, darling. I love you so much, you're my baby. You know how much I love you?

Ellie Not enough. Too much.

Gail There's no such thing as too much love. My therapist said there can't be too much love between a mother and child.

Ellie Surely that depends.

Gail On what?

Ellie On what type of love it is.

  Pause.

Gail These messages it leaves. (*Beat.*) It looks like your handwriting.

Ellie It doesn't.

Gail It does.

Ellie You just think that, because . . .

Gail Because what?

Ellie Because of what it writes.

  Gail lights a cigarette.

Gail I'd cut down. I'd cut down before this.

Ellie Can I have one?

  Her mother gives her one. She lights it. Inhales, exhales.

I fucking hate this house. (*Beat.*) You'll be pleased anyway.

31

Gail What? Why will I be pleased?

Ellie He's coming over.

Gail He? Your –?

Ellie He wanted to see me, and seeing as I'm never fucking allowed out . . .

Gail Good. (*Beat.*) Good, I'd like to meet him. Thank you. I'll try not to embarrass you.

Ellie Don't be like that. (*Beat.*) His name's Frank.

Gail I once dated a Frank.

Ellie He's a vegetarian.

Gail I have peas in. What about cheesy peas?

Ellie No. A proper dinner.

Gail I'm scared to go to the shop. You go.

Gail rummages in her pocket and produces a handful of coins. Holds them out.

These are all your father left me. Go round the corner. Get something nice.

Ellie Oh, you're not scared about *me* going to the shop, then?

Gail Don't. I'm ill. I'm nervous. I couldn't. (*Beat.*) They've stolen my one pleasure, my one escape from myself. They. Them.

Pause.

Please.

Ellie takes the money and leaves through the front door. Gail pours herself a whisky, and drinks it. A huge crash. Scream offstage. Maria runs in holding a large black vibrator.

Maria That's it, it wants to kill me.

Gail What does?

Maria I'm leaving, I'm leaving.

Gail Don't leave.

Maria It tried to kill me. That wardrobe.

Gail Don't leave. Have a drink.

Maria I am sick of this house.

Gail The wardrobe? Hers?

Maria I am sick of this house, it's the devil's house. (*Puts vibrator on the table.*) I found this in your daughter's room.

Gail I'm sorry, I bought her that. It was –

Maria You! YOU! Sweet Mary Mother of God! Nobody cares what I see. Nobody feels any shame. Affairs, f-words. COCKS. (*Beat.*) I am a good Catholic woman. I fear Our Lord in Heaven. This place has no God. This place is the devil's!

Gail Please, Maria, calm down. (*Beat.*) A rise?

Maria You cannot buy me.

Gail I'm trying to be reasonable.

Maria You cannot buy me. You cannot buy things being okay. You couldn't buy happiness, could you? You couldn't buy. Buy safety, could you? I am not some handbag to buy.

Pause. Points up at the sign: PERVERT.

It got that right, though, it got that right.

Pause.

33

You know what? I can't take this any more, I just can't take it. I resign. I resign from this post.

Gail Fine.

Maria Oh! Oh, that's fine with you, is it?

Gail If you want to resign, I can't stop you.

Maria And I. I won't serve out notice, you can't expect me to. I was almost killed.

Gail Fine, just this week.

Maria No! No, not this week!

Gail Okay. Okay, if you want to be like that. (*Beat.*) I don't trust you anyway, to be honest, these – (*Gestures at* PERVERT.) These look like your handwriting.

Maria You're accusing *me*? After all these years working here?

Gail Yes. *And* the cards.

Maria The cards?

Gail Jealousy. Bitterness. (*Beat.*) Everyone else is ruled out.

Maria You're calling me a thief now, after all these years I slaved for you?

Gail Slaved! You were paid a fair wage for a woman of your ability.

Maria Fair? Fair says who? It's fair for me to have no money to buy my kids presents this Christmas? It's fair that I can't afford anything on those adverts they never stop playing, whilst *you*, you swan around on your arse with your booze and get –

Gail Jealousy, you see?

Maria I did not steal your filthy, stupid gold cards!

Gail Yeah, well, you would say that. You proved yourself quite adept at lying over the years.

Maria Lying for you! (*Beat.*) God help you.

Gail Oh, just fuck off then.

Maria That is a nice thank-you, yes. Thank you, Maria, fuck off.

Gail Oh, and empty out your pockets.

Maria does, clumsily, close to tears.

Maria Fine. Fine!

Pause.

Nothing. See? I'm a good worker.

She fumbles her possessions back into her pockets.

You know what? Maybe I should have written that. Often I think, God forgive me, years ago, maybe. Maybe there were things I should have said.

Gail Goodbye, Maria.

Maria There was a morning I came back, and you hadn't slept in your bed. You had slept in little Ellie's, because of the storm you said.

Gail I don't know what you're implying, Maria, but you can stop it now.

Maria And she was crying and crying. Not normal crying. Crying like someone died. And I told your husband and he said not to worry. It was sure to be nothing. (*Beat.*) But I wasn't sure.

Pause.

Gail Get out!

Maria About my wages.

Gail GET OUT, GET OUT, GET OUT!

Maria Okay. I'm getting out.

> *Maria leaves through front door. Gail sits down. After a few moments she stands up again, takes a cloth and scrubs at the word* PERVERT. *It does not shift.*

Gail I know you're there, watching me. You probably think this is hilarious, don't you? (*Beat.*) Judging me, like some little god.

> *Gail scrubs some more, then gives up and throws the cloth aside. Sits back down.*

It's not fair, writing that. Judging me when I'm not well. Why weren't you here when I was well? I watch myself and I'm, I can't stop myself saying things. Like then, letting her go like that! Idiot. *Idiot.* What are we going to do without her to sort things out?

> *Pause.*

I'm tired. (*Beat.*) Why weren't you here judging me when I was making Ellie sandwiches? When I was helping her with maths? I made her a cake last birthday, a double chocolate thing, it took hours, doesn't that mean anything?

> *The whisky bottle lifts, tilts and pours her another drink.*

Oh, there you are. You.

> *A long pause. Then she begins to sing, quietly:*

Good morning, heartache, you old gloomy sight,
Good morning, heartache, thought we said goodbye
    last night,
I turned and tossed until it seemed you had gone,
But here you are with the dawn.

She necks the whisky. Wipes her mouth with the back of her hand. With more gusto:

Wish I'd forget you, but you're here to stay,
It seems I met you when my love went away,
Now every day I start by saying to you
Good morning, heartache, what's new?

She starts to cry. Ellie enters, breathless, red-cheeked and covered with snowflakes.

Ellie I ran all the way. I bought a pepper and an aubergine. To roast. (*Beat.*) There there.

She walks tentatively towards Gail, who swings and grabs her fiercely around the waist.

Gail My muffin. I love you so much.

Pause.

The world, though! The world!

Ellie strokes her mother's hair.

Ellie There, there, I know, I know.

Gail Maria's left. She hates me. She said horrible things.

Ellie That's okay. We couldn't afford her anyway. (*Beat.*) I'll clean that word off.

Gail Would you? Would you?

Ellie Yes, okay.

Gail Alright.

Ellie Okay.

Gail Good.

Ellie pulls away.

Ellie Dad's late back.

Gail He's upset, we're all upset.

Ellie He couldn't have been . . . ? At the mall, I mean.

Gail Oh no, no. Your dad's not a shop-lover. Not a shopper. Don't worry, jellybean.

Ellie Okay. If you think.

Gail Nothing to worry about there.

Ellie No.

Gail dries tears and smartens herself up.

Gail So when's he coming, this boy?

Ellie Soon, I think.

Gail Shall we make cocktails? How about White Russians? Oodles of delectable, creamy White Russians. You make the best White Russians.

Ellie Okay.

Gail Shall I change my dress? Or do you like this dress?

Ellie Is it new?

Gail Not that new, why?

Ellie The tags. I see your tags.

Pause. She notices the vibrator.

What's this doing in here?

Gail Maria found it. She said it was the devil's.

Ellie (*laughs*) Ha! That's funny.

Gail laughs too.

I'm glad she's gone, old snoop. I always felt like –

Gail I did too.

Ellie Like in some weird way she thought she was superior.

Gail This is nice. I like it when we get on.

Ellie I. I guess I do too.

Gail Girls together.

Ellie Yes.

Gail I'm glad he's coming round.

Ellie Yep. I know.

Gail I just like to, you know. I love you.

Ellie Yeah. (*Beat.*) I know.

Gail When you were born your head was too big, they had to use forceps. (*Beat.*) I almost died. (*Beat.*) And when they brought you to me, you were the most beautiful thing, even then, they say babies are ugly, but you! (*Beat.*) Eyes like sloes. Screaming. Full of anger and life, and your tiny perfect fingers, like peeled prawns.

Ellie Was I?

Gail Oh yes, beautiful.

Ellie But I thought you –

Gail Yes. *Yes.* And that's the awful thing, the thing. (*Beat.*) I was supposed to love you, but I didn't, not straight away. I hated what you'd put me through. I. You were so other, so absurd. Like a little ape. (*Beat.*) I didn't even know you were beautiful. I only realise now that you were, and it's too late, I can't hold you in my arms, I can't cherish you. I missed the bit where you wanted me to be your everything.

Ellie Hey.

Pause.

I know you're ill.

Pause. Looks at tags again, more closely.

It's funny, like your dress says 'Made in Thailand', but. I've seen Thailand on TV, it's such an exotic place. These crazy orchids, and monkeys, and beaches so white they're like. Like washing powder. And. And I know the label means one of those people, one of those women with grits of sand in her sandals and chilli breath and who monkeys are just like – they're as common as squirrels to her – I know that she's stitching hems just like yours in this sweaty factory probably, I know that, but it doesn't seem real. I know it but I don't really believe it.

Gail Like the end of the world?

Ellie Yes, exactly.

Pause.

Exactly like the end of the world.

Blackout.

SCENE FOUR

The kitchen. Gail, Ellie, Bob and Frank are sitting around the dinner table, eating roasted vegetables and peas, and drinking Tequila Sunrises. Ellie is wearing a skimpy top, with a cardigan over it. Through the window, which is open, we can see a clear sky, with a low, frosty moon. Bob is visibly troubled and tearful.
PERVERT *is still on the wall, and* CUNTS *has joined it.*

Bob Alright, I guess. Alright.

Pause.

Better with a steak with it. Nice piece of lamb, but. (*Beat.*) Alright.

Frank My mum inspects slaughterhouses. She doesn't eat meat. (*Beat.*) If you saw, if you saw what they do, she says. The conditions –

Bob That's alright, I. (*Beat.*) Rather not know.

Frank She says there's like, you know. *Shit*. Everywhere.

Gail This is a nice Tequila Sunrise, darling!

Ellie Cheers.

Gail I like Tequila Sunrises, they're. Fun.

Bob I needed a drink, I can tell you.

Gail There, there.

Bob The world is just so –

Gail Sorry about the. The graffiti, Frank. She's probably told you about our little –

Frank The poltergeist. Yeah. It's cool, I want to see it. (*Beat.*) I wanted to come round all week to see it.

Gail Oh, you think it's cool? Well I guess it is cool, in a way. (*Beat.*) Is there anything you need, Frank? Salt? Mayonnaise?

Frank Oh, no. I'm okay, I think. It was mad today though, wasn't it? Hard to think it's real.

Ellie Frank's cousin knew one of the shop assistants, Mum.

Gail Is that right, Frank?

Frank I think it was her holiday job. They just found her head. Mad.

Gail How awful!

Frank I know. It looked like a film though, didn't it? Totally mental.

Ellie Frank's totally into movies.

Gail Really?

Frank Yeah, I love them. I watch like, literally a hundred a week. (*Beat.*) So what does this ghost do, then? Just swear and – drop things?

Gail I think it's after me, I think at night –

Bob Darling. You're ill.

Gail Haunted, sweetheart. Haunted. It curls next to me, hands clasped around my throat.

Ellie Once it pulled a wardrobe down on top of our maid.

Frank On your *maid*? That's properly mad!

Ellie We used to be rich.

Bob Please, honey, the *day* I've had. (*Beat. To Gail*) I tried to call my mother, about that. What we were talking about. But I couldn't get through. I'm worried.

   Pause.

Gail She's right, Frank. We used to be rich. I used to go shopping for, oh – all sorts of marvellous, gorgeous things, and. (*Beat.*) That's gone now, I suppose. Goodbye to all that. More peas, Frank? Top up?

Frank Oh, I'm pretty full, thanks.

Ellie We could eat upstairs, Frank.

Frank Oh. Okay, if you like.

Ellie We could watch the news. Do you think there'll be another war?

Frank There should be, I reckon.

Bob Darling, do you have any – any cold meats, or something?

Gail No, no, you two, don't go escaping upstairs, I've got pudding planned and everything. Stay here. Together. (*Beat.*) It's safer together. Come on, my lovely daughter, mix us up some . . . some what? What do you think?

Ellie Whatever. I dunno.

   Pause.

Gin Fizz?

Gail Yes. I like those. I'd like that.

   They all put down their knives and forks. Ellie stands and begins to mix at the side.

Tell me then, Frank, tell me all about yourself.

Frank I. I play in a band.

Ellie Drums.

Gail Drums, really?

Frank They needed a drummer.

Gail So, you've got good rhythm?

Frank It's okay, I guess. It was pretty mental actually – this mate of mine Tony's the singer, real nutter. He said, have you ever played the drums? And I said, er . . . no. And he said, well you better practise then, because I've just made you our drummer.

Gail And is that what you want to do with yourself?

Frank Nah, just a hobby. I don't know what I want to do really. My dad says accountancy's good money.

Gail Oh, you've a head for figures have you, Frank?

Frank Dunno, really. But my cousin's an accountant in New York, he says he'd help me out. (*Beat.*) I was going to ask actually, if, well. I just thought of it in the car, but you work in the city don't you, Mr –

Gail Oh, call him Robert. Call him Bob!

Frank Erm. Bob. I was wondering about maybe. Doing some work experience in the summer. Just to get something for my CV, my cousin reckons anything would help.

Gail Are you listening, Bob? He's asking you something.

Ellie I think that's a really crap idea.

Frank Oh. Why?

Bob I, I don't think I'll be there, to be honest, Frank. Not after today.

Gail I don't suppose Ellie's told you, Frank, but I'm a poet. Was. Was. I've won prizes, but now. (*Beat.*) It's dried up, I can't. (*Beat.*) Now.

Bob It'll come back, it always comes back.

Gail Once one of my poems was in a film! (*Beat.*) You can be my work experience boy if you like. Decant my daiquiris and answer my fan mail. It could be a laugh.

Frank I write like lyrics, you know. For the band.

Gail That's interesting, Frank! I love lyrics. I sometimes wish I wrote lyrics. Music's so much more . . . sexy, I suppose, than the other arts. Physical. I love dancing. How about you?

Frank I'm not great, actually.

Gail Nonsense. It's not about knowing moves, it's about – expressing yourself. Expressing yourself through the body. (*Beat.*) I'm sure that all you need's a good teacher.

Pause. Ellie pours out the cocktails.

Ellie Gin Fizz. Mmm.

Bob Good.

Frank Cool. Gin's the bitter-tasting one, right?

Ellie Yeah, it grows on you, though.

Pause. Gail takes a swig of Gin Fizz.

Gail I love cocktails, they're so frivolous!

Frank Yeah, they're good. In bars they're too expensive.

Gail Bars? Oh, you're –

Frank No, not yet.

Gail You're the same grade?

Frank I'm. I'm seventeen. (*Beat.*) Car.

Gail Oh, of course.

Frank Fake ID.

Gail Oh. Right. And where does a boy your age get hold of that? Do you buy it off immigrants on the black market or something exciting?

Frank Just this bloke at school. Dave.

Ellie God, Mum, you're so naive, you think we don't go to bars?

Bob You shouldn't be in bars.

Ellie Why not? You let me drink.

Bob In moderation.

Ellie You don't care how pissed off my tits I get.

Bob Actually, maybe you've had enough now.

45

Ellie Yep?

Bob Perhaps.

Ellie necks her cocktail and slams the glass down. Refills.

Ellie I don't. I don't think I've had quarter enough. I've not even begun to forget who my father is.

Gail necks hers and slams down.

Gail Why not? I'm in. (*Beat.*) Fill me up too. This might be fun.

Bob Can you not?

Gail And how about you, Frank?

Frank Oh. I'm okay. School night.

Gail Oh, come on, loosen up. You're not an accountant yet. Cigarette?

Bob Do you not think? (*Beat.*) People died, I thought. God, you want to have a party? A bit of respect.

Ellie Dad, I've got a *guest*.

Frank So. This ghost, does it . . . speak?

Gail Only to say 'CUNTS'.

Ellie Mum.

Gail I've been meaning to ask, Frank, how long have you been dating my daughter?

Ellie Don't, just don't, let's be . . .

Gail Well, Frank?

Frank Dunno, a. About a month I guess. We met at the cinema, didn't we, El?

Pause.

46

Gail A whole month? She's a lucky girl. (*Beat.*) Really, a month? That's interesting. (*to Ellie*) Maybe you can remind me, darling, what was I doing a month ago when you were necking with Frankie boy here?

Ellie I don't know, Mum, what *were* you doing?

Ellie removes her cardigan to reveal cuts on her arms.

Bob Do you want to put that cardie back on, darling?

Pause.

Ellie I'm hot, thanks.

Bob You should maybe cover your arms.

Ellie Oh, you've noticed have you? You've noticed my arms after six months.

Bob Just. Cover them, could you? My day –

Ellie And what about you, Mum?

Bob Don't show off.

Ellie Did you never notice my arms?

Gail I was respecting your privacy. I thought you didn't like me snooping.

Ellie Oh. Really? That's really what you thought, is it? Well maybe that's what I thought last month, you fucking HYPOCRITE.

Gail How dare you talk to me like that in front of a visitor?

Ellie Fuck off, you ugly old WITCH.

Pause. The tablecloth is whipped off the table, bringing with it all the plates and glasses in an almighty crash and clatter. They scream, and jump and stumble back from their chairs.

Bob For GOD'S sake!

Gail FUCK.

Bob The. Bloody hell.

Frank Christ. (*Beat.*) That was mental! (*Beat.*) How mad was that? That was the *ghost*!

> *Pause.*

Ellie That's funny.

Gail It's not funny. Our. The best plates. Our *things*, Ellie! (*Beat.*) Is it you?

Ellie Me! (*Beat.*) Look at my hand. It hurt my hand.

Frank It doesn't attack people though, right?

Ellie It cut *me*. Ugh. I think there's glass in it.

Frank It hurt you? Do you need some kitchen towel?

Ellie The fucking cunt cut me!

Bob *Don't* f –!

> *Pause. Ellie sucks the blood off her fingers.*

Gail Being a bit hypocritical yourself aren't you, Ellie? Making such a fuss. The poltergeist's only saved you a job. (*Beat.*) Wish we hadn't had peas now. They've rolled everywhere.

Ellie ARE YOU THERE? COME OUT, COME OUT, WHEREVER YOU ARE! GO ON, CUT ME SOME MORE, I LIKE IT!

Bob Don't. (*Beat.*) Stop.

Frank Yeah, maybe you should stop, El. Maybe you should stick it under the tap.

Ellie HERE WE ARE, COME AND GET US! COME ON! WHY WAIT WHEN YOU CAN FUCKING FINISH US OFF!

Pause.

Bob What a mess.

Gail I know.

Bob But this – this morning I mean. The mess. Thousands dead buying our products. Lured in by our ads. The one with the girl and the snow and the . . . her jugs.

Ellie Her what? Her WHAT? I'm going upstairs.

Gail No you're not, sausage, you're helping me and your dad clean up. (*Beat.*) Maybe you'd like to hear a poem whilst we tidy, Frank. Shall I read a poem?

Frank Yeah, I guess. Cool. Did you want to get a plaster, Ellie?

Ellie No, Mum, he doesn't want to.

Gail He said it would be *cool.*

Ellie He's *polite.*

Bob Well, at least someone is. (*Beat.*) I'm too tired for this, I'm going to watch TV, where's the TV guide?

Ellie There's nothing on.

Bob Oh?

Ellie Just the same pictures, over and over. (*Beat.*) BOOM!

Bob Can you just? The day I've had.

Ellie That and pictures of city centres all over, like ghost towns. The shops all shut. The crossings turning, red to amber to green, and no cars. (*Beat.*) Everything slowly whiting out with this layer of frost, this blankness. Like the world's already forgetting us.

Pause.

Bob So no one knows where the TV guide is, then? Good. Thank you, everyone.

Gail Keep your hair on.

Bob I expect they'll lay me off tomorrow. I expect I'll go in and they'll say ten minutes, clear your desk, and have someone walk me out. Security. (*Beat*) Remember that summer, two years ago? The perks? That waxed-up Mercedes. Those long, liquid lunches, hundred-quid wines, passing the port afterwards. Big fat steaks, and a bill like a developing nation's national debt. (*Beat.*) Those were the days. Me in my new suit, out on the town. Evening, sir. Lap dance. Treated like, like kings. (*Beat.*) I'd bring you back a bunch of flowers every day.

Gail Nearly every day. Yes.

Bob You say I don't hold you enough. I used to then, though, didn't I? We were okay then. I just. Just don't feel like being touched now.

Pause.

Gail Yes.

Pause.

I need a slash.

Gail exits.

Ellie Christ, Dad, can you just. Keep your breakdown to yourself, just for tonight? Does no one care I've got a guest? It's like you're all *trying* to ruin my entire fucking life.

Pause.

Can you at least fucking *answer* me?

Bob They're SACKING me, Ellie.

Ellie So, you'll get another job.

Bob Come on now, don't pretend with me, sweetheart. Your mother might think that, but not you. You're too smart for that. (*Beat.*) Did I tell you they're taking our things on Tuesday? They said they'd be round at three. They sounded like thugs. Not to be messed with. (*Beat.*) They sounded like we should pencil it in.

    Pause.

Ellie I bet they won't take everything. I bet they'll leave the TV.

Bob Maybe.

Ellie I bet they're just saying it to frighten you.

Frank That's pretty mental.

    A flush. Pause. Gail enters, wiping her hands on her skirt.

Gail What's that? Don't listen to what Ellie tells you, Frank, she's a drama queen. (*Beat.*) I tell you what, before we tidy, how about dessert. And for our next course, monsieur and madame, we have – (*to Ellie*) – your favourite, choccy ice cream.

Bob I'll have a bowl.

Gail Ice cream! We're addicts in this house, Frank. Us girls *adore* it. A tub in one sitting –

Ellie Only a little for me.

Gail A little? (*Beat.*) You left most of your meal too. (*Beat.*) Come on, for God's sake! It's a treat. Enjoy. Who knows how long until – (*She gets ice cream out of the fridge and begins spooning it out.*) This isn't another of those dreary teenage cries for help, is it? Anorexia's been done to death, darling, it's not going to impress me.

Ellie I'm just not hungry.

Gail Just sulking. Frank? A big sweet mound for you, I imagine? A growing young man like you. Now where was I?

Pause.

Oh, poems, poetry. (*Beat.*) I've been trying to write one about the poltergeist. But there's just these couple of lines in my head, that's all:

How can I sleep, kitchen,
above your violent puppet show?
When there's a next spring clean,
will I now be the first to go?

Do your knives dance the dark
like girls in silver at a ball?
Do plates grin huge cracked smiles,
to know they're useless when they fall?

Ellie Leave it, Mum, you're embarrassing me.

Frank I liked the bit about the knife. Like a girl. That's a metaphor, yeah? We did them at school.

Gail I'm famous for my metaphors. (*Gail doles out the ice cream.*) Ice cream. I. Scream. (*Beat.*) God, I want to get drunk. More booze. Is there any more Gin Fizz, darling?

Ellie I'll make some more, I guess.

Pause.

Gail There's a lime in the fridge to cut. (*Beat.*) Or shouldn't I let you cut things now? You might not be able to resist, after all, that urge to turn the blade on your poor pasty puppy fat, and write '*Woe is me*' or '*Help*' or '*I am a fifteen-year-old stereotype*' or something.

Bob Just. Please, darling. Not now.

Pause. An owl hoots.

Frank Does that mean it's late? Maybe I should be getting off.

Pause.

Ellie Oh. (*Beat.*) I thought you were staying.

Frank The weather. (*Beat.*) It was fun, though, you know. I mean, it's been totally cool, but. The roads might be death-traps tomorrow.

Gail Well, they might.

Ellie Stay.

Pause.

Frank Nah. I think I definitely should be, you know. Making tracks.

Blackout.

SCENE FIVE

All the kitchen furniture has gone, and Ellie and Gail sit on the floor, picnicking on cheese and wine. Gail is eating chunks of Brie off the blade of a large kitchen knife. Through the window we can see a dark, stormy sky. Wind and rain can be heard lashing the house throughout. PERVERT *and* CUNTS *are still on the wall, and* HELL, LOSERS, DEATH, SCUM, FUCKFACE *and* TWATHEAD *have joined them.*

Ellie (*screaming*) HE FUCKING DUMPED ME, YOU FUCKING CUNT-FACE HAG.

Gail Boys come and go.

Ellie I really LIKED him. He liked me too until –

Gail He probably just didn't want to commit.

Ellie I really, really LIKED him and you RUINED it.

Gail Men always say that. It's not you, I'm just not ready to commit. (*Beat.*) Want to sow their wild oats.

Ellie He fucking DUMPED ME because of you and your nasty, snide comments and your stupid dumb weird –

Gail I wasn't the one turning my arms into road maps.

Ellie I can't believe you just said that.

Gail What, you thought it was a turn-on?

Ellie Don't you care?

Gail Of course I care.

Ellie Bullshit.

Gail He's just a bloke. (*Beat.*) I know! I've got it. He was after your money. He was after your things and then, when he heard –

Ellie FUCK. OFF. I HATE YOU.

Pause.

Gail But listen.

Pause.

You see? Nothing but the wind. There's no one else.

Ellie begins to sob violently.

There there. There there.

Gail places a hand on her shoulder. Sidles closer and kisses Ellie's head.

You're so beautiful. I could eat you.

Pause. Sings:

Good morning, heartache here we go again,
Good morning, heartache, you're the one who knew
    me when –
Might as well get used to you hanging around.
Good morning, heartache, sit down.

Stop haunting me now –
Can't shake you no how,
Just leave me alone –
I've got those Monday blues,
Straight through Sunday blues –

Thunder and lightning.

There, there.

Pause.

You know it's funny, pumpkin, I thought I'd be lonely if
your father ever left me, but then he left, and I didn't
miss him at all. (*Beat.*) I wasn't even slightly lonely until
they came and took our things. Isn't that funny? (*Beat.*)
More wine? Here you go. (*Tops up the glasses, and raises
hers.*) Cheers. To the future. To us. To the weather. To the
weather. (*Drinks.*) The tree in our garden at the moment,
have you seen it? (*Beat.*) The leaves are yellow, this most
gorgeous buttery yellow, tumbling down, and at the same
time, the branches are cramped with blossom. Isn't that
amazing? All this perfect white blossom at the same time.

Ellie I've seen it, yeah. (*Beat.*) It's beautiful.

Gail Isn't it? (*Beat.*) Come on, Sad Sack, buck up. Don't
let the bastards get you down. (*Touches the floor.*) Dirt.
Dust. I never realised how much dust. All the skin we
shed. (*Beat.*) I miss Maria.

Ellie I'm lonely.

Gail lights up a cigarette.

Gail I know, but you've got me, you've got your mother.

Ellie It's not the same.

Gail We can be happy.

Ellie No, Mum.

Gail We can, I know we can, I've got it planned.

Ellie Stop it.

Gail Listen. Listen. (*Beat.*) First I'll look for a job on a magazine, writing about fashion or make-up or something fun like that – I mean, with all my prizes! (*Beat.*) And then we can find a flat, a – a girl's pad, you know, and have parties, you can have such parties. Not like when your dad didn't let you. They'll be cosmopolitan, and chatter, and laughing until dawn, and probably we'll get free clothes and make-up from my job – (*Beat.*) We'll have fun. Won't we? You and me, kid. (*Beat.*) You and me.

Ellie I read in the paper. They're calling this the age of solitude. The eremozoic age. Because pretty soon all the birds will be gone. Butterflies. I mean, the red admirals have already gone from our garden, haven't they? And the goldfinches. Soon it'll be toads. Foxes. (*Beat.*) Then there'll just be us, alone. People and our things. (*Beat.*) It frightens me. (*Beat.*) Everything getting old. Diminishing. The earth diminishing.

Pause.

The age of solitude.

Gail Nonsense, nonsense, your dad always told me, and I *believe* him –

Ellie I know.

Gail You think things'll change but.

Ellie I know.

Gail You think the world's going to end, but it doesn't. You wake up expecting the bomb, the big bang, and there's nothing, there's just some celebrity shagging another celebrity behind some celebrity's back, and they were ten-times-a-night-tastic and coke fiends, or they're trying to raise our taxes again – another blow to the middle classes – or the trains aren't working. Listen, honey, the trains are NEVER working.

She offers the cigarette to Ellie, who takes it. Inhales, exhales.

Ellie I'm leaving you.

Gail No you're not, gumdrop, you're not, you've nowhere to go.

Ellie I'll find somewhere.

Gail You can't though, I need you.

Ellie I need to go.

Gail I'll kill myself. I'll end up back there. (*Beat.*) I'll end up back where I was last month, in the asylum, strapped up, gagging, the loonies goggling at me, no curtains, no forks, it'll kill me, I'm your mother. (*Beat.*) Please I beg you, I'm your mother.

Ellie You can't keep doing this it's NOT FAIR.

Gail I'M FUCKING ILL.

Ellie So? So I'm supposed to ruin my life?

Gail Ruin it? You're supposed to LOVE me.

Ellie NOT. My. Fault.

Gail Maybe I'll try to stay out of your way more, give you more space.

Ellie I have to leave.

Gail You can't let me go back. Please. They put me in these – just these cheap outfits that could have been anybody's. (*Beat.*) Do you have to be so *nasty* to me?

Ellie Me? (*Beat.*) You're *so* selfish! You don't love me. You never loved me. You didn't love me when I was a baby.

Gail I told you, I told you, I.

Ellie You weren't interested in me until I was old enough to dress like a doll and recount your nightmares to. Until I was old enough to know about the eggshells and what I could and could not say to my delicate mother, and that it was my responsibility to look after you and say: 'Oh Mother, I love you so much, you're so talented, Mummy, you're so beautiful –'

Gail I've always been interested in your stuff, always asked about –

Ellie The wrong stuff. Only my boyfriends. Getting off on it. Wanting secondhand kicks 'cause you're a dried-up wrinkly old slut who's –

Gail Shut up shut up SHUT UP.

Ellie NO NO NO I HATE YOU I HATE THIS LIFE I HATE THIS WORLD I HATE YOU.

The windows fly open, deafening thunder, lightning, wind howls into the room. They leap to their feet.

Gail Oh God oh God.

Gracefully, as though part of a ritual, the knife lifts up and hovers in the air. It is radiant. It moves towards Gail's throat. She shuts her eyes.

The kitchen knife oh God oh God oh God oh God shit fuck help.

It reaches her throat and, when in place to cut it, stops. Her eyes open. In reflex she tilts her head back, exposing the length of her throat.

Please put it down, please, please, I don't want to. I don't want it to slit my throat.

Ellie I don't want to die either. Me. But we're going to, aren't we? It's over, Mum. Who are we fooling? Have you seen the weather? (*Beat.*) Have you seen the fucking weather?

  Pause.

I sometimes think about how you must have been, you know, when you were my age, and had this whole life stretching ahead of you. You'd marry a man, and there'd be children, two cars in the drive. A perfect little house, family dinners with roast potatoes. Holidays in Spain, where you'd swig sangria, blinded by the dazzle of chlorine. Savings. A pension.

  Pause.

I want to live as long as you. I want to see this future in front of me where things just get better and richer and cleaner. But it's fucked. It's all FUCKED. What do you give me? Five years? Ten? It's not FAIR. Can you not recognise it's not FAIR?

  Pause.

Have you seen the fucking WEATHER?

Gail Oh God, it's going to kill me. Please please call it off.

Ellie I don't control it. HEY POLTERGEIST, LEAVE MUM ALONE!

  Pause.

See?

Gail I'm scared.

Ellie LET HER GO NOW, JOKE'S OVER!

Gail I've pissed myself. Please.

Ellie I don't control it.

Pause. Ellie is visibly having to prevent herself from sobbing. Tears glaze her cheeks.

Don't panic. Perhaps we can reason with it.

Gail Yes?

Pause.

Ellie *I* was scared.

Gail When? When, my baby?

Ellie When I was young, and Dad was away for a convention or something, on one of his trips, and there were storms like this.

Gail Yes.

Pause.

Yes. We'd both get scared, wouldn't we?

Ellie Yes.

Gail And I'd come to your bed, wouldn't I? To cuddle. So we wouldn't be so scared.

Ellie Yes, you'd come to my bed.

Gail To hug.

Ellie And I'd be scared because you'd come to my bed. And you'd wait.

Gail I waited?

Ellie Because you'd wait until you thought I was asleep, and then I'd feel you.

Gail Please . . .

Pause.

Ellie Rubbing.

Gail Please . . .

Ellie Breathing funny and I didn't know.

Gail Just holding you, that's all. Just love.

Ellie I didn't want to know.

Gail Just loving you.

Pause.

Ellie It was like a bad dream.

Gail Was. *Was* a bad dream.

Ellie It was a metaphor.

Gail I don't remember –

Ellie Please, Mum.

Pause.

You had all the power, and you took what you wanted from me. You took and you took.

Pause.

Gail Please, don't. I'm sorry. I'm so sorry.

Pause.

I love you.

Ellie I don't believe you.

Gail I know, I know, but it's still true. I really do love you, more than. More than all the world.

Ellie walks towards her. Carefully, slowly, she grasps the handle of the knife, but does not move it from Gail's neck.

Is it you then, my beautiful daughter?

Ellie Yes, it's me.

Pause.

Gail I thought it was. And is it over now?

Ellie Yes. Yes. It's over.

Blackout.